Wet and Dry

ELIZABETH LAIRD

Educational Consultant: **Carole Ritchie**

Illustrated By **Clare Beaton**

A Piccolo Original
Piccolo Books

This series has been prepared in consultation with the Pre-school Playgroups Association.

Wet things and dry things

Susie's helping with the washing up.
Billy wants to help too.
He tries to put the salt in the water.
Dad catches it just in time.
'Some things, like salt, mustn't get wet,' says Susie.
'Goo,' says Billy, licking the salt off his fingers.

'Yes,' says Dad, 'and some things, like Billy's tongue, are always wet.'
'Ugh,' says Billy, trying to spit out the salt.

Can you see some things in the picture which are always wet, and some which are always dry, and some which are sometimes wet and sometimes dry?

Some things mustn't get wet

Billy's been busy again.
He's put a bit of bread in his milk,
and it's gone all soggy.
Now he's just about to tip some
water into the bag of flour.
Dad will have to be quick if he
wants to save it.

Some things spoil if they get too dry

Susie's growing cress seeds on wet kitchen paper.
They've grown quite tall already, but she forgot to water them yesterday, and they've flopped over today.
'Don't worry,' says Mum. 'Water them now, and they'll soon straighten up again.'

Billy hid some of his breakfast yesterday. He's always crawling about with some food in his hand, then hiding it, and forgetting it. The bread has gone hard, and dry, and crusty.

Can you see any other things that would spoil if they got too dry?

Washing the clothes

Mum's put the washing machine on.
Billy watches the soapy bubbles
froth up and the dirty clothes
go round and round.
His eyes go round and round too!
The dirt floats off the clothes
into the water.

Have you ever tried washing
clothes in soapy water?

Now Susie's playing with bubbles.
She mixes some powder paint
with warm water and a little
washing-up liquid.
She blows the bubbles through
a straw. Pop! They burst and
leave a lovely pattern.

Could you do that?

Drying the washing

The washing's done, and now
it must be dried.
Sometimes, Mum hangs it out
on the balcony, but today she's
drying it indoors.
The water in the clothes slowly
turns into a kind of mist
and floats off into the air.

Now it's Billy who needs a wash.
He's been eating a banana.
What a mess! Susie washes him
and dries him on a towel.
Now *he's* dry, and the towel's wet.
Susie puts it in a warm place to dry.

Where do you dry clothes at home?

Eating and drinking

Susie and Billy have been at the playground. Susie has been chasing some of her friends. She's hot. Her face is wet because she's sweating, and she's very thirsty.
'Do you want something to eat?' asks Mum.
'No,' says Susie. 'I just need a drink!'

You need a drink when you're thirsty, and you need something to eat when you're hungry.
Which of these things can you eat,
and which can you drink?

Wet sand and dry sand

Susie and Billy both like playing in the sandpit. Billy likes it best when it's dry because it trickles through his fingers and pours easily and because he can push his hands right into it. The only trouble is, he tries to eat it sometimes.

What do you like doing with dry sand?

Susie likes playing with sand when it's wet because she can dig in it, and build with it, and shape it, and turn it into things.
The only trouble is, it sticks to her hands when she tries to eat an apple.

What do you like doing with wet sand?

Feeling wet and feeling dry

Susie's been playing in the paddling pool.
The water was so nice and cool!
It tickled when it trickled down her back.
But now the sun's gone in, and it's got chilly.
Susie's shivering with cold because she's wet.
'Quick, Mum! Where's the towel? I'm freezing!'

It's fun playing in the water, but it's nice to be dry most of the time.
Look at all these things we use to keep ourselves dry.

Can you think of any other things we use to keep ourselves dry?

Bathtime

Billy has been playing
with his boat in the bath.
He pushed it under.
It came up again with a plop!
Do you like doing that?

Susie let her flannel soak up lots
of water, then she squeezed it out,
and watched the drips.
Do you ever do that?

What else do you like doing in the bath?

Dad has dried Billy and put a clean nappy on him.
Now Billy will be warm and comfortable in bed.
Susie's very good at drying herself,
but Mum helps her with her pyjamas.
Susie and Billy are both ready to go to sleep.
After all, it's been a busy day.

Try it for yourself...

What happens when you make these things wet?

Fill a bowl with warm water.

Put in: a piece of toilet paper
Does it fall to pieces if you try to lift it out?

a piece of kitchen towel
Does it soak up the water?

a scrap of coloured paper from a magazine
How long does it take before it goes soggy?

Now put a teaspoon of salt into cold water and stir it around. Can you still see it or does it disappear?

Water soaks right through some things, and runs straight off others.

Which of these things soak water up?

Sponges soak up lots of water. Can you empty a bowl of water just using a sponge?

Put the sponge in the water, then take it out and squeeze it in the sink. How many squeezes do you need before the bowl is empty?

Here's something else for you to try.
Wrap some cling film over and round
a plastic pot.
Gently pour some water on to it.
Shake the drips off,
and take the cling film off.
Is there any water in the pot?

Now put a damp dishcloth over the plastic pot.
Gently pour some water on to it.
Take the dishcloth off.
Is there any water in the pot?